# *Letter to* DONALD TRUMP

## MAKE AMERICA RE-GRET AGAIN?

# VIVIEN YOUMBI

Copyright © 2024 Vivien Youmbi.

All rights reserved. No part of this book may be reproduced, stored, or transmitted by any means—whether auditory, graphic, mechanical, or electronic—without written permission of both publisher and author, except in the case of brief excerpts used in critical articles and reviews. Unauthorized reproduction of any part of this work is illegal and is punishable by law.

ISBN: 979-8-89419-301-4 (sc)
ISBN: 979-8-89419-302-1 (hc)
ISBN: 979-8-89419-303-8 (e)

Because of the dynamic nature of the Internet, any web addresses or links contained in this book may have changed since publication and may no longer be valid. The views expressed in this work are solely those of the author and do not necessarily reflect the views of the publisher, and the publisher hereby disclaims any responsibility for them.

One Galleria Blvd., Suite 1900, Metairie, LA 70001
(504) 702-6708

# Contents

Introduction ............................................................................... 1

My personal beef with President Trump ....................................... 3

Why did you turn into a "shithole" president that day? ............... 13

Why don't you ever apologize? ................................................. 17

Donald Trump and his narrative identity ................................... 21

Why do people like Trump? ...................................................... 25

Be Authentic ............................................................................. 29

Donald Trump's Invincibility, The Universe,
    and The Law of Attraction .................................................. 37

Trump and the power of the subconscious mind ........................ 41

Donald Trump and the gift of persistence ................................. 49

Donald Trump always takes the road less traveled .................... 53

We all deserve a second chance ................................................ 57

Bibliography ............................................................................. 61

# Introduction

The world has always been running on divisive thoughts, polarizing politicians, who tend to create severe tensions between people who naturally or organically, will love each other. Political campaigns are a perfect example of this phenomenon, where they tend to denigrate or tear each other down in order to gain the attention or sympathy of the public or potential voters. Needless to remind you that politics runs on popularity, and any behavior or action that will increase a politician's popularity will be emphasized. I would like to inform all actual readers of this book that this book is not about a politician; It is not about promoting an ideology or a political party philosophy. It is not even about celebrating the win of a candidate, or a political party over another. This book is about finding the best in us. It is about transcending obstacles and turning negative situations into our advantage.

We might not like Donald Trump or his business practices, but I am pretty sure we all admire his bounce back attitude, resilience, and his fightback spirit. Both being vital ingredients necessary for navigating through the un-masterable labyrinth of life. Life being a permanent fight, each of us need to be like a boxer in a ring; always keep our guards up. That is exactly what Donald Trump exemplifies, and that is what I am celebrating in this book.

I first wrote Letter To Donald Trump published in 2018. It was a reactionary book due his derogatory comments on African countries that he then called "shitholle countries". Years have passed, campaigns have been run, some lost and others won, January 6th happened, lives have been lost, Trump has been both at the offensive and defensive, facing at this exact time (as I am writing these lines) 91 criminal offenses in four criminal cases. Politicians have not deviated from their constant inconsistencies and lies. And now, we are in the process of electing another president. All these above-mentioned facts are symptomatic of the classic political game, where "We, The People", mean nothing at all. Confirming the old say about politician fighting for their own ambitions or their party's interests. Oh, yes! Politics has always been about the next elections, not the next generation. The next generation being forgotten while the next election is prioritized.

All the above-mentioned facts have triggered the need or necessity to understand the "TRUMP Phenomenon" as he is making another run to get back into the White House. It is therefore my personal obligation to share my thoughts about the winning attitude of President Trump, and explain how he won the 2016 presidential elections, and how by the same process, he will shock the world once again in the next presidential elections.

It is my sincere hope that this book brings more clarification and understanding to those who want to know more about President Trump, and above all, that we all learn not to be politicians, but to use Trump's approach to daily life's attacks for our personal growth and benefits; because "the story of one person is the story of everyone, and one man's quest is the quest of all humanity" (Paolo Coelho)

I promise not to quiet anything to please some people, nor say something to hurt or disrespect others.

# My personal beef with President Trump

*You are certainly wondering how I got myself involved in a beef with the president of the United States! Well, this is the story: In January 2018, then President Trump made a shocking remark (that I called attack) on several countries among which some located in the African continent. His statement that made global headlines referred to Haiti, El Salvador and other African countries as "shithole" countries. Until then, I had never been involved in personal attack, nor was I interested in politics (I have always believed that politics is a fixed game, and all politicians are all liars and lack character). Calling people from other nationalities "shithole" people triggered a sense of revenge and responsibility into me. I felt the need and obligation to respond because it was a direct attack on poverty and social class. I felt so ashamed because I had always shown a "don't care" attitude when other nationalities where attacked.*

*when Donald Trump called Mexican people
rapists and drug dealers, where was I?
He called them rapists, murderers, and drugs dealers;
I did not open my mouth because I was not from Mexico.
He called them pigs and I laughed; I thought it was funny.
He called an athlete "son of a bitch";
I kept quiet because I was not a professional athlete.
And when he made the statement about "shithole"
countries, I knew he was coming for me.*

*When he looked down on women, why did I not say something? Where was my sense of general humanity? where was my human sensitivity? where was my cultural empathy? I immediately remembered Martin Niemöller with his famous, deep and significant quote:*

> *"They first came for the Socialists, and I did not speak out because I was not one;*
>
> *then they came for the Trade Unionists, and I did not speak out because I was not one of them.*
>
> *then they came for the Jews, and I did not speak out because I was not one of them.*
>
> *then they came for me, and I couldn't find anyone to speak out for me".*

*Out of frustration, shame and guilt, I decided then to write a letter to President Trump that I published in a book in 2018, and that can be summed up in the following lines:*

*Mr. President.*

*Calling African countries SHITHOLE is un-dignifying, and it robs us of our human values. But there is something that eases my mind about SHITHOLES: we do not care about our buttocks until it's time to sit down. No matter how dirty a SHITHOLE is, we know it is important.*

*The simple thought of being treated as such triggers so many questions as suggested by most of the people I spoke with about the issue.*

*I wonder how I will be looking at my people when I go back to my native Cameroon, or how I will be looked at by those same people. Clearly, the question is how they will be looking at me knowing that even though I was insulted and denigrated, I still want to return to the United States? I am sure*

*I will have an answer for them. I will tell them you are a good man. And my question to you Mr. President is this:*

*Should I agree with them?*

*Should I believe all the people who think that you would have been among those who initiated some denigrating and cruel experiments in people you considered "SHITHOLE" and of low value?*

*No! I do not want to believe that.*

*Should I believe that you would have been part of those who initiated the Tuskegee experiment, the Jim Crow Law, the Cherokee Trail of Tears, the Nazi medical crime, the Willow brook study, or the Guatemalan venereal disease experiment?*

*No! I do not want to believe that.*

*They even added that Ebola was another experiment done on SHITHOLE countries especially in Africa; but I refused believe it.*

*Should I believe that you share the same thoughts as President Thomas Jefferson when he disturbingly said about Black people "they smelled bad and were physically unattractive, required less sleep, were dumb, cowardly and incapable of feeling grief". (3) Maybe that is why you compared African nations to SHITHOLES.*

*No! I do not want to believe that.*

*Should I believe that you could have been one of those who wrote the Virginia Code of 1705 in order to dehumanize people brought from Africa in America by protecting slaves' masters who punished slaves by killing them?*

*No! I do not want to believe it.*

*Even if this Virginia Code specifically stated that "and if any slave resist his master, or owner, or other person, by his or her order, correcting such slave, and shall happen to be killed in such correction, it shall not be accounted a felony; but the master, owner and every such person so giving correction, shall be free and acquit of all punishment and accusation for the same, as if such accident had never happen".(4) This is perhaps why police brutality has been very accentuated lately in this country. But I want to believe otherwise Mr. President. Even though some stories and fact about the 1920s "klannists" suggested otherwise, I still don't want to believe the fact that police brutality is co-signed by those who are supposed to protect citizens; "in fact, their lynching rested on widespread white consent and the open collusion of law-and-order officials" (5).*

*Did you not overtly say during the campaign: "I am the law-and-order candidate"?*

*Should I believe that in the name of science, you could have given a Prize to Doctor Marion Sims, who in the mid-1800 performed the first vaginal speculum? "Sims built a makeshift hospital in his backyard where he conducted surgical experiments on countless un-anesthetized African slave women" (1), justifying it by saying that African women, because of their race could sustain any type of pain.*

*Had you been a Eugenist, would you have supported Madison Grant and Lothrop Stoddard in their "campaign to encourage greater fertility among the "superior" class and to discourage fertility among the inferior class"? (5)*

*No, I do not think so.*

*Had the Trump University survived, would you have made it mandatory to study Eugenism?*

*No, I do not think so.*

Mr. President: we all know that you are smart and pride yourself in saying it. You have outsmarted all information/media specialists by forcing them to accept your way of communicating. You have become the tweeter in chief, and this ability to always getting what you want inspires me a lot. You are a persistent man. You once said, "it's my way of life, for better or for worse".

I have read some of your books even before you signed your lease at 1600 Pennsylvania Avenue NW in Washington, D.C. in January 2018. I was-and still am- one of your biggest fans. Never apologize for your greatness is one of the boldest and daring advice I learned after reading two of your books: **The way to the top** and **Think big and kick ass in life and business**.

But Mr. President, there is no rules without exception. Do you still stand by that theory? Will you not apologize to SHITHOLE nations? Please make me proud by doing so; make me proud by keeping your words of apologizing in a distant future if you are ever wrong, as you told Jimmy Fallon when interviewed by him: "I think apologizing is a great thing, but you have to be wrong...I will absolutely apologize, sometime in the hopefully distant future, if I'm ever wrong" (33). I believe you were wrong calling African countries SHITHOLE countries, and they deserve some honest apologies from you. They deserve it because "we must be ready to apologize when an apology is appropriate and helpful" otherwise, we will have to believe that "the inability to apologize is directly related to our feelings of inferiority... certainly, part of our difficulty with apologizing is the problem we have with interior honesty" (6).

I truly don't believe you have feeling of inferiority, nor an interior honesty issue Mr. President.

Had you been a writer, would you have written **An essay on inequality of race**? the book that legitimized racism and in which aristocrats are considered superior and more important than regular people? Would you have said like its author J, Gobineau (July 14th 1816 – Oct 13th 1882) that *"niggers strangely resemble cows; do they have their power and strength? I don't know. But niggers certainly have their slowness".*

*No, I don't think you would have said that because that period coincides with the birth of your grandfather Friedrich Trump born in 1869 in Germany. Even though your father Fred Trump concealed his German origin, you were courageous enough to carry the pride of your German origin. Coincidently, the first African slaves who arrived in the United States in 1619 were transported by a Dutch ship. Long story short Mr. President, those slaves/niggers from SHITHOLE countries started working to prepare your father's arrival here in the United States. I do not think those slaves were doing office jobs, or intellectual jobs, nor even management ones. They were SLAVES doing what White men could not do. I don't know what immigration status Fred had when he entered this country, and it really does not matter because we are proud to have a President who is an immigrant's descendant. What really bothers me is that despite your immigrant indirect origin, you are not cool with immigrants and "SHITHOLE" countries. Apparently, you are cutting down on legal immigration. Just remember that "SHITHOLE" countries built the foundation of America and immigrants are its soul. Educated or not, poor or rich, from SHITHOLE countries or not, immigrants are a great asset to America Mr. President. Think of the snowball effect of their participation in the economy:*

*How many of us work in jobs we consider mundane and relatively meaningless, never considering all the good we are actually doing? Whether we are blur collar workers or white, work for the minimum wage or for the big bucks, rarely do we pay attention to all those we are truly helping. The administrative assistant to a claim adjuster at an insurance company is one of a long line of folks that help others recover from their losses...the important question is: are you aware of all the people that depend on them? And we haven't even spoken about all the good they do, providing for their family. (1)*

Mr. President, those slaves made you wealthy and today, you are calling their progeny SHITHOLE while all they want is reap the benefits of what their ancestors sowed more than two hundred years ago. Calling them SHITHOLE angers us just like progeny of slaves are constantly living in a state of anger. "Anger at living in the wealthiest nation in the world and not having equal opportunity and access to its riches" (1). The fact of the matter is that "246 years of protracted slavery guaranteed the prosperity and privilege of the south's white progeny (like you) while correspondingly relegating its black progeny (like me and other African-American) to a legacy of debt and suffering" (1). Yes Mr. President, African-American communities are suffering and are in debt here in the United States, SHITHOLE countries are suffering and are in debt. Matter of fact, my country of origin was listed as POOR and OVER-ENDEBTED COUNTRY. That is the reason why we are here, working on bettering our lives and that of those who cannot make it here. By doing so, we are relieving you from sending financial aids to developing countries. That is how we give a meaning to our lives; knowing that "the greatest task for any person is to find meaning in his or her life" (7). Help us fish, do not feed us. Like the alchemist of Paulo Coelho, we want to transform led into gold, and we definitely need your cooperation. The more SHITHOLE countries send their people in the United States, the less pressure the United States is going to feel. SHITHOLE countries do not send their people here because they are weak, but because they want to become strong. The other side of the story is that most of us are here because we have to be here, and we are paying the price of adventuring in America. Verily, none of us wants to be here. America robs us of our culture and traditional values. America created more problems (psychologically) than it solved for immigrants. In fact, "the path to psychopathology can begin almost immediately for immigrants. Upon arrival into a country, they are bombarded with discriminatory messages from the dominant culture…perceived racism can cause mental health symptoms similar to trauma and can lead to physical health disparities" (8). Some of them have to undergo multicultural counseling sessions in order to adjust and fit in the American Way of Life. I know what you are thinking and are about to say Mr. President. "You made the choice". That is another topic.

*Should I believe that you are a heartless man when you allow parents to be separated from their children by deportation? And DACA recipients facing deportation as well? Are you aware of the Post Traumatic Slave Syndrome Mr. President?*

*No! I don't want to believe that because you are such a great father and wouldn't allow any child to be raised without enjoying the presence of their parents. I am sure you really don't want DACA (Deferred Action for Childhood Arrivals) recipients to miss the American Dream. Just like you taught Ivanka the magic and admirable touch of business, those children would love to learn from their parents as well. Did you not learn your business skills from your father? You started learning from him at five years old. He taught you everything you needed to know in order to succeed, and you learned everything very well.*

*Speaking of DACA and non-documented immigrants, something needs to be done and I believe you will let them stay. If you don't, will you not be participating and encouraging "the systematic effort to destroy the bonds of relationships that hold them together, as well as continuing efforts to have them believe themselves to be less than human"? (1). Allowing those families to be separated would be the validation of what Linda Gordon describes in The Second coming of the KKK. In fact, she compares these types of behaviors to "Governmental actions that created a model for the Klan's fight to exclude the "wrong kind" of people from belonging in America...The Klan argue not only for an end to the immigration of non- "Nordics" but also for deporting those already here. The date of their immigration, their longevity in the United States, mattered not" (5).*

*Speaking of KKK, it appears that your father Fred was arrested at one of their riots in 1927. When asked about this topic few years ago, you stated "This never happened. Never took place. He was never arrested, never convicted, never even been charged. It is a completely false, ridiculous story. He was never there! It never happened. Never took place" (9).*

*And I do not believe it is true either.*

*I am just bringing this issue up because the same people told me that KKK is coming back, and, just like you learned real-estate from your father, you could have adopted KKK's principles as well. But I think it is total BS. They are not telling the true. You would never do that. Even though some priorities of your administration coincide with that of the 1920s Klan's priorities especially immigration restriction, I tend to deny the fact that there is a connection with KKK. Stephen Miller is playing the role of "Klan member Albert Johnson of Washington who served as chair of the House Immigration Committee and led the drive for immigration restriction" in the 1920's. Microaggressions, resurgence of White supremacists, police brutalities, and opposition to immigration are some of the characteristics of The Second Coming of the KKK; as described by the author of the book who happens to be a historian. But what is history other than a narrative giving the perception of whoever writes a history book? Based on this Mr. President, I personally don't know what to think about* **The second coming of the KKK**. *What do you think?*

*Mr. President.*

*I am going not going to mention all absurdities I have been told and heard about you, because I don't believe any of them. I still believe you are a good man; and want to make America great again.*

*One recommendation Mr. President: as you are running for another term in 2024, make sure you do not make America Regret again like you did after the events of January 6th.*

January 6th, 2021

Mr. President,

# Why did you turn into a "shithole" president that day?

> *Violence is the last refuge of the incompetent.*
>
> —*Isaac Asimov*

*January 6th has become a historical landmark in the United States of America. Needles to make a narrative of events that day, as it is engraved in our minds. Regardless of the claims of victory given by Trump and his team, we all come to an agreement: the events of January 6th were an assault not only on democracy as a concept, principle, and tradition, but also an insult to American history. I personally believe that it ranked second after the burning of the White House by the British troops on August 24th, 1814.*

*Wanting to use an antidemocratic tactic to remain in power was both shocking and surprising to the whole world. The Unites states of America is viewed as the perfect model or example of power alternance or democracy in the entire world. Your attempt to hijack the elections reminded some of us about strategies used by "shithole" countries presidents in order to remain in power. In fact, you legitimized their permanent desire to stay in power. If the teacher cannot preach by a perfect example, how can students learn? How do you think you were looked at by all shithole countries who believed in the power of democracy, and the influence of the United States of America in the world? How will you be remembered by all political science students? Thomas Jefferson, George Washington, Benjamin Franklin, Alexander Hamilton, John Adams, and James Madison are certainly saying: what the hell is going on back there!*

*Mr. President, was that Carma getting back at you? If it was, I encourage and urge you to learn from that day (January 6th) and never allow such an event to be repeated in this country.*

*Mr. President, by attempting to force your stay in the White House, you infringed one of the symbolic signs of true democracy, which is the peaceful transfer of power to the upcoming president. In fact, you behaved as a true politician, instead of being a true leader. Dr Myles Munroe clearly defined leadership not as a sprint, but a relay marathon where the passing of the baton should be a moral imperative, thus allowing democracy to live. Unlike in "shithole" countries where most presidents refuse to pass the baton, it is a tradition in American democracy to voluntarily pass the baton, allowing democracy to meet its true essence, which is power alternance.*

*What will be your legacy? what will future generations say about you? Should I agree with the psychologist Mc Adams when he stated that unlike any other president in modern times, you have virtually no sense of history, and absolutely never talk about things like "prosperity" or "legacy" or how "future generations" will look back upon the America of today?*

*I sincerely hope your second coming into the White House gives you an opportunity to make things right by peacefully transferring power to whoever wins in 2028.*

Mr. President,

# Why don't you ever apologize?

> "I think apologizing is a great thing, but you have to be wrong...I will absolutely apologize, sometimes in the hopefully distant future, if I'm ever wrong".
>
> —Donald Trump

In a civilized society, it is of good action to say "I am sorry" to those we hurt or deceive. Our society recognizes apologies not as a recognition of mistake, but more like acknowledging the superiority and preeminence of the relationship over oneself. That is why it is said that apologizing does not always mean you are wrong and the other is right. It just means you just value your relationship more than you value your ego. What happen to our ego then? Should we deny ourselves and please our society to whom we own strict respect of rules and norms? Isn't it a way of denying or ignoring our true self? Apologizing is a form of self-punishment, a sense of auto-destruction. Shouldn't we value the relationship with ourselves more and better than we value the relationship with others? Yes, we should. I should not apologize just to please the society and others. That is once again Donald Trump. A man who never apologizes; be it in politic or in business.

I have heard people complain about the fact that Donald Trump never apologizes. Well! Welcome to Trump's Island: Trump never apologizes. That should probably be the title of his next book. Once again, that is the Trump's way. What does he think about that? "I think apologizing is a great thing, but you have to be wrong…I will absolutely apologize, sometime in the hopefully distant future, if I'm ever wrong" (29).

Few years ago, as President Obama was touring the world and attempting to rebuild the image of the United States of America as most people thought Americans were not welcome overseas, Donald Trump thought it was not a good idea. For him "we should not apologize for our greatness".

Donald J. Trump is sometimes criticized for bragging about his financial achievements, and I think they are wrong. First, no one can deny that he is rich; and secondly, why should he not say it loud? I think that claiming loud his riches is a way of thanking the Man above or the universe. Some religious people call it gratitude. There is a verse in the bible that seemed wrong and unfair to me years ago. But as time went by, I understood that verse and it makes more sense to me now. "For whosoever hath, to him shall be given, and he shall have more abundance: but whosoever hath not, from him shall be taken away even that he hath" (30). In one word, if we have something and we pretend not to have it, that thing will be taken away from us. In return, if we show that thing to the world and express our gratitude of owning it, we will be given more. And that is the psychology behind the attitude of Donald Trump. He is said to worth 8 or 9 billion dollars today. All those riches are attracted and accumulated through the constant repetition of its proclamation. This is one of the positive traits I do admire about Donald Trump. As I said in my introduction, this book is not about a politician; it is about a man who transforming led into gold like the alchemist of Paolo Coelho, it is about a man teaching us personal development tools. Any psychologist or personal development expert will mention the power of repetition.

The famous law of attraction teaches us that we tend to attract to us what we talk and think about all the time. Therefore, it is not an accident if Donald Trump is proud of himself and claims as loud as he does all the time.

On December 14th, 1987, Donald J. Trump was asked by the host of the Phil Donahue Show "you shouldn't have called Mayor Ed Koch a bad name; don't you want to take it back? That is bad PR". To which Donald J. Trump responded: "no I don't take it back. When it comes to running the city, he is like anybody I've seen. Ed Koch has been a disaster for the City of New York" (31). And that is the Donald that American people discovered during the campaign. Verily, it is not a new trait of character for him. He has always been the man who never apologizes.

I do not believe Donald Trump will ever change. I do not encourage him to do so. It is part of his true self, part that has taken him where he is today. Part of his narrative identity.

# Donald Trump and his narrative identity

*Narrative identity takes part in the story's movement, in the dialectic between order and disorder.*

—*Paul Ricoeur*

*Narrative identity is one element upon which I found my belief that Donald Trump will win back the White House. I simply define narrative identity as the way some events repeat themselves in someone's life. In an interview given to North by Norwestern, Mc Adams educates us on the theory of narrative identity when he says that "beginning in adolescence, people start to become historians of the self. People begin to see their pass as something that they can make meaning out of, and reconstruct it in a way that helps them understand where they may be going in the future". (North by Northwestern).*

*Unless I am mistaken, narrative identity is about the story of ourselves, our personal lives. As such, there is no standard qualification or fixed principle to judge one's life's story. I am therefore surprised when some people argue that Donald Trump has no narrative identity. Amongst those, the psychologist Mc Adams stated that Trump is an episodic man, "living forever in the combative moment, striving to win each moment, moment by moment, episode by discrete episode". He added that "the past has no purchase on him, and the future has no pull. Instead, he lives in the exuberantly combative moment, fighting like a boxer to win the round, fighting furiously as if it were the last round he will ever fight" (The strange case of D T). Well, let us stop right here and make an attempt to comprehend the contradiction brought by this scientist. And this is where I find the story of Trump interesting as it has a didactic approach; instructing or educating us on how to deal with daily life challenges. Why should we worry about tomorrow? Og Mandino wisely told us that "tomorrow is only found in the calendar of fools". Is Trump not a wise man by only thinking about the present and living in the moment? isn't that what performance psychologist advise us to do when they teach mindfulness and the notion of being aware of the present and our surroundings?*

*Why would we want to solve tomorrow's problems today? why should we consider life as a straight continuum where there are no doted lines? why should we live life as a whole instead of a somme of pieces? We all heard of the famous say LIVE ONE DAY AT THE TIME.*

*Professional athletes talk about the importance of focusing only on the process and doing each task right, without focusing on the outcome or result. As a sport psychologist, one thing I know is that focusing on past mistakes or future results steals energy from the most important moment of our lives. The most important moment being the present, the now. A wise man once said that yesterday is history, tomorrow is a mystery, today is a present, a gift we should all take the opportunity to do the things we do. And this is exactly why I personally like about Donald Trump. As I mentioned at the beginning of this book, I do want to remind readers that this book is about a man navigating the tumultuous challenges of life and finding ways to overcome them. Remember that Donald Trump is a human with challenges and tribulations as any of us do have. I want each of you to forget about the politician Trump and absorb the wisdom of the fighter Trump. Hence, I will not agree with this statement of Mc Adams': "My reading on his life and his presidency led me to conclude that Trump lacks an inner story to provide his life with temporal continuity, purpose, and meaning"*

*Speaking of his narrative identity, we all know that Trump has faced so many challenges not only in his personal life, but also in his professional life as well; and he has always got out of those challenges miraculously. I do believe that it is to be credited to him leaving in the moment and not focusing on the future. Mc Adams supports this thesis when reminding us that "Trump's total embrace of the moment has always worked to his advantage, both in business and politics". Here comes to the light the crucial question on Trump's behavior: why would we want Donald Trump to change? If he does (which he will never), wouldn't it change the outcome of many things? View as such, Trump will always be Trump, and will always win no matter the obstacles. He is aware of it; he knows that he is the author of his story, and knows that he must not change a winning strategy. Lies, insults, contradictions, exagerations, are just part of his winning process; and it is a solid foundation of his narrative identity. "It does not matter to Trump if what he says today blatantly contradicts what he said yesterday, or what he will say tomorrow". Trump, the stable genius is also aware of the fact that "the same event, can mean very different things for the same person at two different points in time" (Josselon, 2009).*

*Let me be clear here by saying that I am not making an apology of lies, contradictions or other "unacceptable" societal behaviors; nor am I celebrating the "by all mean" philosophy (where we have to use any mean to reach our goal). I am not making an excuse of Donald Trump's behavior; I am explaining how the awareness of the self can help us find our way in life. In spite of Trump facing multiple legal challenges at this time, President Trump is still leading in the pools, and will certainly be the republican nominee. All this is to be credited to his narrative identity and the way he writes his own story by being true to himself.*

*"I could stand in the middle of 5th Avenue and shoot somebody, and I wouldn't lose voters"; "when you are a star, they let you do it. You can do anything. Grab them by the p\*ssy". Needless to remind in what context the above-mentioned statement was made. The question is why is Trump becoming more and more popular in spite of all those inflammatory comments? why hasn't he sunk giving his derogatory declarations? It sadly looks like the more people hate Trump, the more popular he becomes. How possible is it that these types of contradictions participate to his narrative identity mostly made of wins, bounce backs, resiliencies, and political invincibility? We could easily answer these questions if we understand that Donald Trump has always receive favors from the universe. He is just one of those individuals to whom miracles happen, and to whom we cannot give a logical explanation to things that happen to him. Mary L. Trump, in her book entitled "TOO MUCH AND NEVER ENOUGH," describes a story in which Trump was involved in a casino deal with banks in the early '90s, and he was able to escape situations that would normally have sunk any other ordinary person. She says, "the only part of the scenario that defies explanation is the fact that the banks and investors in his first two casinos didn't object more strenuously to his opening a third, which would cut into their own bottom lines" (Trump, Mary). The fact that she talks about a scenario that defies explanation is prove enough that Trump is not an ordinary human being. He has always been favored by the universe.*

# Why do people like Trump?

*Our biggest struggle as human being is to project ourselves as something that society has deemed admirable or likable instead of being honest.*

—*Matthew Shultz*

*In spite of being politically incorrect, verbally abusive, defiant towards the legal system, and all other misbehaviors and deviant attitude that he displays, Trump is still liked by many Americans. How can this phenomenon be explained? I believe it is one of those contrasts that makes the universe functions. Truth be told, nature and the universe functions by strange contrasts, that you, the reader, are too small to understand, and I, the writer, am even smaller to explain. Scientists can attempt to describe, pretending that they are explaining, but they do not. The only Being capable of explaining contrasts that rule the universe is the creator of this universe. Some might call that superior Being the Creator God, others Allah, another Buddha, etc. To me, the most important thing is to acknowledge the fact that there is a super-supra Being, to whom we must all submit and on whom we must depend. Have you ever thought of the right side of our brain being in command of the left side of your body; and vice versa?*

*Why do people like Trump then?*

*If the question was asked to Trump himself, without hesitation, his answer will be: people follow me because I am a stable genius; I am very smart, I am going to make America great again, and so on and so on. ........But if we must explain, we can either let science intervene, or enter the field of personal development.*

*If science were to give us an explanation, it would be summarized in the following paragraph.*

*In an attempt to explain "what attract people to Trump and what is their animus or driving force", the president of the world mental health coalition Brandy X. Lee explained it by two factors that could once again play in Trump's favor this year in the upcoming presidential elections. The first factor is listed as narcissistic symbiosis referring to "developmental wounds that make the leader-follower relationship magnetically attractive. The leader, hungry for adulation to compensate for an inner lack of self-worth, projects grandiose omnipotence- while followers, rendered needy by societal stress or developmental injury, yearn for a parental figure" (Tanya Lewis, the shared psychosis of Donald Trump.*

*The second factor is the "shared psychosis", also referred as "madness for millions". According to Lee, this "refers to the infectiousness of severe symptoms that goes beyond ordinary group psychology". He follows by stating that "when a highly symptomatic individual is placed in an influential position, the person's symptoms can spread through the population through emotional bonds, heightening existing pathologies and inducing delusions, paranoia and propensity for violence- even in previously healthy individuals" (Lee, 2021. Shared psychosis of Trump..........). And here we have a clear scientific reading of the dirty event of January 6th. Needless to remind you all episodes of the disastrous assault on the Capitol.*

*The second element that can explained Trump's attractiveness is his authenticity.*

# Be Authentic

*To be yourself in a world that is constantly trying to make you someone else is the greatest accomplishment*

—Ralph Waldo Emerson

"I wish to stress that the true meaning of life is to be discovered" (7). I personally believe that in order to discover oneself, we need to be free. We live in a society where rules, regulations, policies, and protocol are master words. We are expected to act according to what society thinks is good and acceptable, in order to maintain the status quo among its members. It is in fact a polite prison that all of us enjoy living in, agreeing to take part at its erection. That is what we do when we elect our representatives who in turn design and decide on policies that influence the interactions among us. Going against the tide seems to be a form of rebellion. Going against those rules, laws and regulations is absolutely forbidden, and as consequences, we face punishments, sometimes the individual can be subjected to some form of ostracism. In such society, we wonder where our true self, our originality, or our freedom is. What should we say, what should we do, or even how should we act? Our freedom is at stake. We worry more about what people think and say about what we do. Our actions are contingent to the public approval or acceptance. Those who act contrary to the rules of the society are called deviant. The question here becomes: how should we express our uniqueness and originality? Will we be accepted when we act authentically? What look will we receive when we tell the truth about who and what we are? And the true question now becomes can we be happy if we cannot be ourselves? How can we freely act in a rigid society? They feel oppressed in these circumstances, as they know that "fully human people accept what they are, physically, emotionally, and intellectually. They know that what they are, as far as it is known to them, is good; they know that their potential selves are even greater". (6). For them, not being free of being themselves is synonym of oppression. And we all know that what is suppressed must be expressed one way or another. It is like a balloon or ball that is continuously inflated; at one point, it will explode. Let us keep in mind that in the pursuit of happiness, one key element is the importance of following one's dream with passion, and that letting our emotion being part of that quest is a key element. If we do suppress that emotion, our passion loses its power, and we lose interest in our dream, which means we will be living a lifeless life. Perhaps that is why Benjamin Franklin said that many people die at age 25 and don't get buried until they turn 75. Do you wonder what happen between 25 and 75? I will tell you right away: they slowly kill themselves with stress and diseases they get from regrets, excuses, and bad choices they have made like not being true to themselves. In the field of psychosomatic medicine, it is well known "that repressed emotions are the most common cause of fatigue and actual sickness". Those repressed emotions usually express themselves in the form of rashes, headaches, allergies, asthma, back pain, and other. All these little aches or diseases combined, contribute to lowering and destroying our immune system. Consequently, the body starts eating itself, and this is what I call auto-psychological cannibalism.

How can we protect ourselves against this self-inflicted disease called auto-psychological cannibalism? By inviting originality and uniqueness into this trip called life.

"If I want to be free, I have to be ME," said Bill Gove. But in truth, who is ME?

> Me is who I am
> Me is the person who is true to myself
> Me is the person in me, displaying his originality and uniqueness
> Me is the person who conceal his similarities.

Being who we are, being true to ourselves, displaying our originality and uniqueness, concealing our similarities is the key here: "it is not only much more conducive to feelings, but equally essential to our integrity and health" (6). To which I add that it also helps build our confidence, self-esteem and release our personal power. Me is the "REAL YOU" who should "stand-up" and tell me who you really are because "when you tell me who you are, when you share with me your uniqueness, you will take me into a different world, a different time and place, a different family" (6). In doing so, you earn my trust and win my vote. ISN'T THAT WHAT

TRUMP DID? DID HE NOT GET THE VOTES OF AMERICAN PEOPLE by remaining unique, original, and true to himself?

Dr. Scott Peck states that "we must be totally dedicated to truth. That is to say that we must hold truth, as best as we can determine it, to be more important, more vital to our self-interest, than our comfort" (12). The most important word here is self-interest. It comes from what we cherish and pushes us to aim towards it. Being true to ourselves releases our personal power and facilitates our social acceptance for those who in return are like us. Joe Magee is an expert on power and teaches at New York University; he explains that "personal power is all about having the confidence to act based on one's beliefs, attitudes, and values, and having the sense that one's actions will be effective." I think that the word EFFECTIVE in that context means getting the result we want. Let's relate this theory to Donald Trump: this man only knows one way; he always fights back whenever he is attacked. With Donald Trump, it is "business as un-usual". One of his advices is "always get even when you're attacked". We have seen Donald Trump during all debates fight back even when he was told the public did not like that. He was told to act presidentially when facing other democratic presidential nominees; but the man kept being himself. That is the Trump's way, that's the way he knows and does his things. Like he said in one interview: "It's my way of life, for better or for worse". He was told to be uncharacteristic and not holding good manners when interrupting other candidates; but he did not care! He kept being Donald Trump. In fact, Trump says it like it I, without putting any mask or attempting to sugar coat things. And that is what scores of Americans love. They recognized themselves in the republican candidate, liked him and decided in spite of all "societal misconducts" to push him to the white house. This is what many Americans have said about him in an article found in the McClean's Magazine on September 26th 2016:

> "I like his anti-political politeness"

> "Trump may be crude and offensive, but he is authentic"

"I almost support all of his statements, because they are not politically correct, they are mostly the honest truth"

"He is a businessman/entertainer- not a politician at all. He, therefore, makes remarks that could be considered offensive to some"

"I can appreciate honesty, even when I don't particularly love the way in which the honest ideas are delivered"

"Maybe you only agree with 80% of what he says. But at least he is being direct and not just pandering to some middle road like every politician."

"Combined with a considerable gift of humor (which may also be aggressive), anger lies at the heart of Trump's charisma. And anger permeates his political rhetoric". Says Dan McAdams, professor of psychology at Northwestern University. Trump must have flirted with one of the greatest athletes of all time named Muhammad Ali who used to say that his way of joking was to tell the truth. Trump always tells the truth his way.

Truth be told, that has always been Donald Trump: outspoken, controversial, fights-instigator. Let's follow David Cay Johnston in his book *the making of Donald Trump*: "Donald was what school counselors might call "maladjusted." In his first book **the art of the deal**, he boasts about slugging his music teacher in second grade because he didn't think the teacher knew the subject, although the story might be apocryphal. Neighbors have told stories over the years, including to me, of a child Donald throwing rocks at little children in playpens and provoking disputes with other kids. By his own account, Donald got into lots of trouble-so much that his father shipped him off to the New York Military Academy in upstate New York to develop discipline when he was a teenager" (13). This is what Donald Trump says about his own character: "Even in secondary school, I was a very assertive, aggressive kid. In the second grade I actually gave a teacher a black eye- I punched my music teacher because I didn't think he knew anything about music, and I almost got expelled. I'm not proud of that, but it is clear evidence that even early on I had a tendency to stand up and make my opinions known in a very forceful way. The difference now is that I like to use my brain instead of my fists." (14). Do we all see here the roots of his temper and behaviors? Of course, we do. McAdams while writing an article in The Atlantic in June 2016, explains this: "A large and rapidly growing body of research shows that people's temperament, their characteristic motivations and goals, and their internal conceptions of themselves are powerful predictors of what they will feel, think, and do in the future, and powerful aids in explaining why" (15).

Regarding what people might call "disrespect" towards women, this also has been the Trump some people discovered during the elections. In 2005, Trump was to give a motivational speech in Colorado on the topic *how to succeed in life and business*. With no rehearsed presentation nor text prepared, Donald Trump kept more than a thousand people interested in more than one hour. Trump told one of the guesses, that happened to be a former employee of his, (who insisted on asking question to ridicule him), that she was "ugly as a dog." Here, I recognize the Trump not using teleprompter and talking "disrespectfully" to a woman. Donald tells things the ways they are! Period. That is who he is, and he is not afraid to tell us who he is. That is the real Trump. John Powell when talking about the "real person" says "in our society, we have placed a great stress on being authentic. We have talked about placing masks over the face of our "real" selves, and of playing roles that disguise our true and real selves. The implication is that somewhere, inside me, lurk our real selves" (16). John goes on to add this: "what you and I really need is to come to a moment of truth and to develop a habit of truth with ourselves. We have to ask ourselves in the quiet, personal privacy of our own minds and hearts: what games do I play? What is it that I am trying to hide? What is it that I hope to win?". (16). Trump knew he was trying to win the white house; he also knew he needed to win being true to himself in the game of politic where so many people play hiding their true selves. Not Donald Trump. Amy Cuddy, a professor of social psychology at Harvard Business school thinks that the notion of being our real self is related to "the knowing and feeling that you are being your most sincere and courageous self. It is autonomously and honestly expressing your values through your actions" (17).

In the end, Trump is Trump; he does thing his way. Be it politics, personal relationship, business, he admits "it's my way of life, for better or for worse" (34).

Jeffrey Lord makes the case for Trump when he gives seven reasons why this country needed Donald Trump. Among then, he said "America needs a truth-Teller" (18). Which goes along what Ivanka Trump said referring to her father: "My father is not politically correct, he says what he means, and he means what he says, and I think that is the way the American people are". Donald Trump usually capitalizes on this fact. He knows with John Powell that "fully human people accept what they are, physically, emotionally, and intellectually. They know that what they are as far as it is known to them, is good; they know that their potential selves are even greater". He goes on to say that the greatest kindness someone has to offer you is always the truth.

To the question (which happens to be the title of his book as well) "why am I afraid to tell you who I am?", John Powell answers like most people would by stating: "because if I tell you who I am, you may not like who I am, and it is all that I have". In the case of President Trump, he is not afraid of telling things the way they are, telling the truth. Donald Trump is behaviorally organic and natural; and that is exactly what most Americans like in him.

This leads me to extent my point on Trump's model of life: always be yourself in whatever endeavor you find yourself into. Do not change your true self. Do not copy what other people do because, by doing so, you lose your identity, and in losing your identity, you lose your sense of purpose. If there is no purpose, why are we alive? When human beings get to that situation in life, they are living their greatest tragedy. The late Dr. Myles Munroe always reminded us that "the greatest tragedy in life is not death, but life without a reason. It is dangerous to be alive and not know why you were given life" (In pursuit of purpose).

# Donald Trump's Invincibility, The Universe, and The Law of Attraction

*There is a gold mine within you from which you can extract everything you need to live life gloriously, joyously, and abundantly.*

—Joseph Murphy

*The universe in which we live functions by laws. One of the laws that has always been misunderstood is that of attraction. This law says that if you vibrate in harmony with anything or any person, you can attract that thing or that person towards you.* One thing we should know is that the law of attraction functions both ways: in negative or positive way. We can attract good things, or we can attract bad things. So, depending on what we put in our mind, we will get a consequent output. President Trump has benefited from that law in 2016 and will receive the same support in November 2024. The law of attraction does have a secret: it does not literally operate according to our wishes, but according to how we express it. When we say we do not want something to happen to us, usually that unwanted thing does happen to us. Have you noticed that whenever you say for example that I don't want to arrive late at work or at school, you usually arrive late? This is why: by some strange mechanism, the universe does not capture the negative part of the sentence; it does ignore or cancel it. So, when you say I DON'T WANT TO ARRIVE LATE, the universe usually removes the NOT, and hear this: I DO WANT TO ARRIVE LATE. In the case of Donald Trump in 2016, the majority of American wanted Trump to lose; everyone was against Donald Trump. What played in Trump's favor is how his haters expressed their wishes. They all said I DO NOT WANT TRUMP TO WIN. Remember the trick about the law of attraction? it does always take out the NOT and only register I DO WANT TRUMP TO WIN. So, by wishing Trump loses the elections, people instead were favoring him by sending out messages to the universe. To fully understand this universal law of attraction, I recommend reading THE SECRET by Rhonda Byrne who said that "Often, elections are tipped in favor of the person that the people are really against, because he's getting all the energy and all the focus" (27).

Simply put, we all need to always say to the universe what we want instead of what we do not want. Given that the universe will always give you what you ask, it will give you what you want and ask if you genuinely want it with strong desire and faith. In the Alchemist, Paolo Coelho remind us how strong our will should be for the universe to open doors for us and good things to happen to us. According to him, when you are seriously working on a dream, the universe conspires to make everything become possible. And with Trump in 2016, the universe truly came to his aid. Hillary Clinton's emails put out few hours before election night was the universe acting in favor of Trump. For those who follow sports and particularly basketball, if you remember the 2019 NBA finals opposing Toronto Raptors against the Golden state warriors, Kevin Durant tearing his Achilles tendons was the universe making things happen for the Toronto Raptors, especially for his president Masai Ujiri, who, a year earlier took the risk to trade his best player (Derozan) for Kawhi Leonard who was coming out of a series of injuries.

# Trump and the power of the subconscious mind

*The sky is not the limit. Your mind is.*

—Marylin Munroe

Most people only believe in things they can see, making their physical eyes the only source of belief in their lives. They sometimes forget that there is another element in the constitution of the human being: the mind. Some psychologists refer to the subconscious mind as the most productive part of the human being and advise us to invest in its development. "The subconscious mind is always working days and night" said Earl Nightingale. It should be fed with positive thoughts and desires. Therefore, if we really desire great things in life, we should force our mind to think our way. Donald Trump wrote Think Big in which he declares "I like thinking big, if you are going to be thinking anything, you might as well think big" (19).

In the pursuit of our happiness and dreams, we need to be aware that it is not going to be a cake walk. We will –not might- face challenges and oppositions, and in this constant battle, only the brave and strongest people will see light at the end of the tunnel. Many people give up after a first trial of their project just because they have failed, or they met opposition on their way. Opposition will come in the form of ridicule, not having enough information on what needs to be done, or even being let down by people we counted on. We all fail at one point of our lives, but what really counts is not the fall or the failure. The most important thing is to be able to get back up and continue the battle without accepting being defeated. Easier said than done I know! This, because it requires a superior power that most people refuse to call upon when necessary: our mind. This is the most powerful instrument ever given to us by the creator of the universe, God, Allah, or any other connotation according to our religious orientation. If the mind gave us any materialistic items on earth (bombs, weapons, buildings, cars, airplanes, computers), how can it not take us where we want to go! Sure, it can, and it will. "Doctor Williams James, father of the American psychology, said that the greatest discovery of the nineteenth century was not in the realm of physical science. The greatest discovery was the power of the subconscious mind, mixed to faith. In every human being, is that limitless reservoir of power, which can overcome any problem in the world" (20). Truth be told, we, as human beings are destined to grow every day. I am not talking about the physical growth here. I am referring to our mental and emotional growth. Donald Trump understood that principle and clearly stated where he was going: to the top. Perhaps that is why he wrote *the way to the top* twelve years ago. Success truly starts with a mindset. By designing and showing where we want to go, we are expressing our faith and believes towards our goal. There is more than what we see with our physical eyes in life. We must rely on unseen forces says Price Pritchett: "when you focus constantly on a clear picture of what you want to accomplish, and move toward it confidently, the unseen forces will rally to your support" (21). There's a reason why the bible tells us to walk by faith not by sight. For Donald Trump he was able to see things that were not there, using his mind. That is called FAITH. Faith that Trump has used in times of hardship. "Faith is a bit like wisdom. People can help you along the way with it but above all you have to develop it yourself. Faith in yourself can prove to be a very powerful force. Work on it daily. Sometimes when you are fighting a lonely battle, keeping yourself company with positive reinforcement and faith in yourself can be the invisible power that separates the winners from the losers." (22).

In spite of all discouragement and critics, he knew what he wanted and was able to focus on his goals. Napoleon Hill says that "faith is a state of mind which may be induced, or created, by affirmation or repeated instructions to the subconscious mind, through the principle of auto-suggestion" (23). Here, we need to stress the term "affirmation" and "repeated instruction". Those two, undoubtedly have the power to create a sense of contagious belief in our environment. By constantly repeating something, people around us, easily and quickly pick up, and magically, even automatically, things start to happen. This technique is well known of greatest and successful athletes who have some notions of sports psychology: by practicing self-talk, we end up making what we talk about happen. That is perhaps why Muhammad Ali used to say that "it is the repetition of affirmation that leads to belief; and when that belief turns into faith, things start to happen". Wonder why he kept repeating to whoever wanted to listen that "I am the greatest". Donald Trump understood this principle, and was able to wisely apply it during his run to the white house. "We are going to win again and we are going to win so much; we are going to win.... win....and get tired of winning". Did he not win? That is the power of the subconscious mind in application.

Well understood and utilized as suggested by Dr. William James, the father of American psychology, the mind, intimately connected to our heart, always leads us to desired results. That is certainly why Paulo Coelho said, "when a person really desires something, all the universe conspires to help that person to realize his dream" (2). With eleven days left before the decisive election date, the FBI decided to reopen the controversial e-mail case of the democratic candidate Hillary Clinton, giving a new momentum to the Trump's campaign: that was the universe conspiring to make Donald Trump's dream come true. Donald Trump's business almost collapsed in the early ninety; but was rescued by the government and banks who thoughts he was too big to fail: that was once again the universe conspiring in protecting him.

The power of the subconscious mind and faith are intertwined: they are life-long partners. They depend on each other to prove their individual power. Speaking of faith, people always ask if Trump has faith at all! "Consider his persona as a businessman who made a fortune in part through casinos, who has bragged about sexual exploits and who has been married three times, Mr. Trump has conceded that people are sometimes surprised to hear him talk about faith at all" (24); to which Trump responded during the campaign: "People are shocked when they find out I am a protestant. I am Presbyterian. And I go to church, and I love God and I love my church". Faith does not have to be connected to religious beliefs; having faith to me is the ability to trust yourself and do what appears to be impossible to Mr. EVERYBODY without knowing how things will be accomplished. Faith recommends trust in ourselves, self-confidence, and a constant positive mental attitude. All we need is to know where we are going; how we are going to get there is none of our business. It is the business of a greater being.

What is the source of Trump's faith? His parents Fred and Mary attended Marble Collegiate church in Manhattan, where Doctor Noman Vincent Peale was the preacher. Whoever is familiar with the personal development industry knows that when referring to Vincent Peale, we refer to POSITIVE THINKING. And that is exactly where Trump started building his character. Doctor Norman Vincent Peale's message is built around the notion of can-do mentality. According to him, each of us can do anything he/she sets his/her mind to do. All we need is believing in our abilities to achieve a project, and always think positive. One of his prescriptions is "utter faith" that he summarizes in these few sentences:

1- create a mental picture of yourself as a success, hold on to this picture tenaciously, and never permit it to fade. Since your mind try to complete what it pictures, always picture success no matter how badly things seem to be going at the time.

2- do not build up obstacles in your imagination; minimize them instead. Problems should be seen for what they are, and never inflated by fearful thoughts.

3- don't be obstruct by other people or try to copy them. Remember that most people despite their confident appearance are often as scared and doubtful of themselves as you are.

4- get a confident counselor to help you understand the origin of your feelings of inferiority and self-doubt. These feelings often begin in childhood. Self-knowledge leads to a cure.

5- each day practice the following information: repeat it out loud it's possible: I can do all things through Christ who strengthens me.

6- make what you think is the true estimate of your own ability, then raise it 10%. Don't become egotistical but develop a whole sense of respect. Believe in your own God release powers

7- put yourself in God's hands. To do that, simply state: I am in God's hands.

You can think your way to success and happiness (25).

Having been exposed to such type of messages very young, we now understand why he is always self-confident and always sees light even when things appear to be depressing. What faith does is that it allows us to build an unshakeable explanatory style, foundation of the paradigm that govern our lives. The explanatory style is composed of three elements with one having a greater impact in the constitution of our personality: PERMANENCE being "the degree to which one feels events will repeat and continue to affect one's life either negatively or positively" (26). By expecting good things to happen all the time, Trump was/is able to make those good things happen. This type of attitude is understood by some writers as the law of attraction which was described in 1912 by Charles Haanel as "the greatest and the most infallible law upon which the entire system of creation depends". Trump's presidential victory in 2016 can be credited to that law; and it probably will in 2024. To fully understand this, I recommend reading THE SECRET by Rhonda Byrne who said in that book in 2006 that "Often, elections are tipped in favor of the person that the people are really against, because he's getting all the energy and all the focus" (27).

We must praise and give credit to his parents who understood the power of exposure on children. That is why I agree with someone that parenting is the most important job in the world, along with coaching and teaching. To which Napoleon Hill adds "it should be recognized as a crime (it is indeed a crime of the worst nature) for any parent to build inferiority complexes in a mind of a child, through unnecessary criticism. Employers who understand human nature, get the best ... not by criticism, but by constructive suggestion. Parents may accomplish the same results with their children" (23).

# Donald Trump and the gift of persistence

*If you can't fly then run, if you can't run then walk, if you can't walk then crawl, but whatever you do, you have to keep moving forward.*

*—Martin Luther King Jr.*

*When a task has begun*
*Don't stop until it's done*
*Be it great, be it small*
*Do it well or not at all*

*—Unknown*

Donald J. Trump was told a story by his father when he was a teen. The father thought it was funny, but the son, Donald took it seriously, and that story had a lasting impact in Trump's life. This is how the story unfolded: "there's a man who wanted to start a coke company and began by calling it 3UP. The company failed. He relaunched the company and called it 4UP, it failed again. He made another attempt and called it 5UP, and he failed again. After the fourth attempt where he named the company 6UP, he lamentably failed and decided to give up. Had he tried only one more time, he would have launched 7UP!" The young and ambitious Donald Trump then understood the power of persistence.

Napoleon Hill in his timeless book entitled *Thing and grow rich* states that "lack of persistence is one of the major causes of failure. Moreover, experience with thousands of people has proved that lack of persistence is a weakness common to the majority of men" (23). The fact of the matter is that in order to persist you must have started somewhere. In the majority of cases, most people won't even start because they listen to their surroundings, ending up killing their dreams and passion. John Mason (28) gives this wise advice: "never surrender your dreams to noisy Negatives". It is a lot easier to take care of this issue when the negative or the enemy is outside of us. The situation becomes critical when the enemy we face is ourselves. There is an African proverb that says if there is no enemy within us, the enemy outside can't do us no harm. So, we need to pass that first test before facing our surroundings. When Donald Trump announced his candidacy in 2015, he was ridiculed by the New York hometown newspaper of June 17th 2015, with this headline: Trump throws rubber nose in GOP ring… "CLOWN RUNS FOR PREZ…" These types of remarks by the press usually discouraged some people; not Donald Trump. He decided to push forward.

As Donald Trump kept pushing his luck during the campaign, some disturbing allegations were thrown at him. Some analysts and political commentators even advised Donald Trump and team to drop out of the race. But Trump is not known to be a quitter. He knew that: "when a task has begun

> Don't stop until it's done
> Be it great, be it small
> Do it well or not at all".

When all polls and predictions gave a double-digit advantage to the democratic candidate Hillary Clinton, he was not impressed and boldly told his supporters and the media "don't believe in polls folks; they mean nothing".

In the quest of happiness and success, keeping the momentum is one important step toward the pursuit of our dreams. Price Pritchett says, "the only way you control your dream is (1) knowing where you're going, (2) continuing the pursuit, (3) learning from your mistakes" (21). The people who really make a difference in this world are those who in spite of all opposition and ridicule, decide to stay glued to their dreams by not taking NO for answer. With the power of persistence, they end up making their dreams become a reality. The Wright brothers with the airplane; Thomas Edison and the light bulb; Karl Benz and the automobile industry, and so many others that I certainly don't know have used this success principle. They all understood the power of persistence.

# Donald Trump always takes the road less traveled

*Two roads diverged in the wood, and I took the one less traveled by, and that has made all the difference.*

*—Robert Prost*

Success in life requires sometimes to take an unconventional approach. Not doing things the way everybody is doing requires courage, faith and boldness. This strategy has always been proven efficient for its devotees. Donald j. Trump has always been part of the philosophy of the solitarian: always going against the tide, and that has been a part of his success strategy. One that is akin that of Arnold Schwarzenegger who always break the rules not the law.

In the early 1990s, there was a building that was for sale and so many agents and representatives were involved in the deal. Instead of dealing with all the people involved in the transaction (Donald Trump called them middle people), Donald flew in a foreign country to meet the owner of the building and dealt directly with him. Which happened to be one of his best deals ever! In fact, 40 wall street a 72-story building downtown Manhattan was purchased at $1000 000 and now worth more than $600 000 000.

We have certainly heard these two phrases countless of times: "<u>But I tell you not to resist an evil person. If someone slaps you on your right cheek, turn to him the other also;</u> if someone wants to sue you and take your tunic, let him have your cloak as well". Well! Sounds like good advices, right? But not to Donald J. Trump. His rule is very practical and simple: always get even and always fight back. The psychology behind that philosophy is that when you fight back, it is not necessarily to teach the person who hurt you a lesson; it's to teach all the people around you that you will always defend yourself. It's the discouraging consequences of your fight that should motivate you to fight back. Once again, Donald demonstrates his ability to be himself even when it comes to religious beliefs.

This philosophy of thinking in the opposite direction has been carried out even in the political arena during the primary, and more importantly during the final race against the democratic candidate. Donald Trump was advised not to campaign in some blue states because they thought he could not do well in those. In spite of those advises, Donald remained Donald.

He went ahead and campaigned in most of those unadvised states with the result that shocked America on the night of November 8$^{th}$, 2016. Michigan, Pennsylvania, Wisconsin and Ohio states turned red that night.

Donald J. Trump understand that in order to make it in this world, we have to make things our way and not follow the crowd. He must have read Ralph Waldo Emerson who said "do not go where the path may lead you, but go where there's no path and leave a trail".

# We all deserve a second chance

*There is some good in the worst of us and some evil in the best of us. When we discover this, we are less prone to hate our enemies.*

*—Martin Luther King Jr.*

"The United States of America, the greatest nation in recent history, has come to a crossroads because of a lack of national purpose" said the late Dr. Myles Munroe. Warren Bennis, professor at the university of southern California added that "America lost its edge because it lost its way. We forgot what we were here for. We talk about freedom and democracy, but we practice license and anarchy". This statement is from his book entitled becoming **a leader.**

John Kasich, the governor of Ohio wrote in 2004 a book in which he invited each American to stand for something in the quest of the American soul. I personally believe it was used by many Americans as a raincheck. And I think it is time to bring it back on the table. At a time when the country is more sundered than ever; at a time when political leaders are no longer models for our youth; at a time when economic challenges and social crisis dictate our daily climates, it's imperative, even mandatory for each of us to reflect on our priorities and decide to be part of the solution. I stand for love and tolerance as these are two greatest assets without which none of us can peacefully navigate in the permanent quest of happiness. We do need each other and that requires love and tolerance. Only the unseen power of those two can help us reclaim the American soul. This country is first and foremost made of people; states are not as powerful as WE THE PEOPLE. WE THE PEOPLE are whites and blacks; straights, gays and lesbians; rich and poor; old and young; handicaps and physically abled; educated and non-educated; Native Americans and immigrants; cutes and ugly; fat and skinny; sick and healthy, desperate and hopeful…etc. No matter where we stand in this picture, it is our human and personal duty to look up to those who are on the opposite side of our status. We need to promote love and tolerance.

In one word, we need to stand for something. I heard someone said that if we do not stand for something, we can fall for anything. Making America great again requires the conversion of the United States of America into the United People of America; as we must learn to live together or, together we will drown.

Will America give Donald Trump another chance to reconquer the White House? It is all up to each of you. As for me, I wanted to explain how an individual can turn obstacles into assets. Once again, I am not for violence or defiance to law; I am just describing how we can all navigate the tumultuous labyrinth of life, and more importantly, what type of mindset each of us need to conquer and reach our goals. One of the things we must first do is to be ourselves. The Trump's way of life is an invitation to call upon ourselves to stand up and claim our authenticity like John Powell commands us, "Will the real me please stand up!".

# Bibliography

1- Degruy, J. (2005). *Post Traumatic Slave Syndrome: America's Legacy of Enduring Injury and Healing.* Portland, OR: Joy DeGruy Publications Inc.

2- Coelho, P. (1993). *The Alchemist.* New York, NY: HarperCollins Publishers.

3- Peterson, M. The portable Thomas Jefferson: Notes on the State of Virginia, 1781. New York: Viking Press. 1975. Pp.192-193

4- State of Virginia Casual Killing Act, 1669.

5- Gordon, L. (2017). *The Second Coming of the KKK: The Ku Klux Klan of the 1920s and the American Political Tradition.* New York, NY: Liveright Publishing Corporation.

6- Powell, J. (1985). *Will the Real Me Please Stand Up?* Allen, TX: Tabor Publishing.

7- Frankl, V. (1959). *Man's Search for Meaning.* Boston, MA: Beacon Press.

8- Norcross, J. & Prochaska, J. (2014). *Systems of Psychotherapy: A Transtheoretical Analysis.* Stamford, CT: Cengage Learning.

9- Extracted from: https://www.washingtonpost.com/news/the-fix/wp/2016/02/28/in-1927-donald-trumps-father-was-arrested-after-a-klan-riot-in-queens/?utm_term=.472d07e0a73c

10- Peck, S. (1978). *The Road Less Travelled: A new psychology of Love, Traditional Values, and Spiritual Growth.* New York, NY: Simon & Schuster.

11- David, J. *The making of Donald Trump.* 2016. Brooklyn, NY: First Melville House Printing.

12- Trump, D. & Schwartz, T. (1987) *The art of the deal.* New York, NY: Random house publishing.

13- Extracted from: https://www.theatlantic.com/magazine/archive/2016/06/the-mind-of-donald-trump/480771/

14- Powell, J. (1998). *Why Am I Afraid to Tell You Who I Am?* Allen, TX: Thomas More Publishing.

15- Cuddy, A. (2015). *Presence: Bringing you BOLDEST SELF to your BIGGEST CHALLENGES.* New York, NY: Hachette Book Group.

16- Lord, J. (2016) *what America needs.* New York NY: Regnery Publishing

17- Trump, D. & Zanker, B. (2007). *Think Big and Kick Ass in Business and Life.* New York, NY: HarperCollins Publishers.

18- Murphy, J. (2007). *The Power of your Subconscious Mind: unlock your master key to success.* Radford, VA: Wider Publications, LLC

19- Pritchett, P. (2012). *YOU$^2$: A High Velocity Formula for multiplying your personal effectiveness in Quantum Leaps.* Dallas, TX: Pritchett & Associates.

20- Trump, D. & McIver, M. (2008). *Trump never give up: how I turned my biggest challenges into success.* Hoboken, New Jersey: John Wiley & Sons, Inc.

21- Hill, N. (2008). Think and Grow Rich. New York NY: Penguin Group.

22- Extracted from: http://eds.a.ebscohost.com/eds/detail/detail?vid=3&sid=3b668975-9f85-440d-96cb-64ab7a211810%40sessionmgr4009&hid=4210&bdata=JnNpdGU9ZWRzLWxpdmU%3d#AN=118398691&db=f5h

23- Peale, N. (2003). The Power of Positive Thinking. New York NY: Touchstone

24- Byrne, R. (2006). The Secret. Hillsboro, OR: Beyond Words Publishing

25- Mason, J. (2013). An Enemy Called Average. Tulsa, OK: Insight International, Inc.

26- Extracted from: "Donald Trump on Tonight Show: The good, The bad, and The delusional," by Jessica Roy, TVGuide.com, September 12, 2015

27- All KJV are extracted from the New King James Version of the bible.

28- Phil Donohue extracted from: https://www.youtube.com/watch?v=q8-TBT1_8bY

29- Extracted from: https://www.theguardian.com/us-news/2015/sep/12/donald-trump-on-the-tonight-show-i-will-apologize-if-im-ever-wrong.

30- Extracted from: https://www.npr.org/2017/01/20/510680463/donald-trumps-been-saying-the-same-thing-for-30-years Source: Donald Trump, by Glenn Plaskin, Playboy, March 1990

31- Trump L. Mary. (2020). Too much and never enough: How my family created the world's most dangerous man. Simon Schuster, New York, NY.

32- Tanya, Lewis. (2021) Extracted from The 'Shared Psychosis' of Donald Trump and His Loyalists | Scientific American https://www.scientificamerican.com/article/the-shared-psychosis-of-donald-trump-and-his-loyalists/

www.ingramcontent.com/pod-product-compliance
Lightning Source LLC
LaVergne TN
LVHW042245070526
838201LV00088B/35